Music and Family Life
Tudors, Stuarts, and Georgians

Alison and Michael Bagenal

Music Department
OXFORD UNIVERSITY PRESS
Oxford and New York

Oxford University Press, Walton Street, Oxford OX2 6DP, England

Oxford is a trade mark of Oxford University Press

Contents

Cassette available
ISBN 0 19 321028 2

Acknowledgements

Illustrations by Shirley Tourret
Design by Creative Intelligence, Bristol.

Pull-out Pages
(between pages 22 and 23)

Introducing the
Three Families

You will meet three imaginary families from the past, a **Tudor** family, a **Stuart** family, and a **Georgian** family. For each family and their household, there is selected music from the relevant period, and additional activities are suggested to bring the people to life. The aim is to provide **ideas and materials for in-depth classroom projects on the social life of these periods.**

How to Use this Book

Role-play is an excellent way to learn about other people's lives, so a list of roles is provided for each household.
■ Decide together which role each person will play. Some will prefer to work in pairs. Examine together the picture of your family's house, and discuss each person's function and activities in the house or its surroundings. There is information about each family to read aloud.

Dramatic situations are included for each section of the book in the pull-out pages. These are mere outlines: the more you learn about the families, the more vivid and imaginative your role-play will become. You will be able to extend the open-ended situations provided in your own way, and the children may prove unexpectedly inventive.
■ Use these suggestions for drama work in the classroom, or for a history day, or for a visit to a historic property (see the list of properties on the inside back cover). Conversations may be improvised or scripted as you prefer.

Music and dances from each period have been chosen to illustrate characters, e.g. *The Highwayman's Song* and *A Tune for a Jester*, and to express the mood of a social occasion, such as a dignified *Pavane* for a Tudor banquet, and a lively country dance for a Georgian harvest home. All the music has been arranged simply for classroom instruments. In addition there are opportunities for **creative music-making**, e.g. devise a sound picture for the Great Fire of London.

■ Encourage musicians to provide appropriate backing for the melodies to emphasize their character. On page 5 there are more practical hints for using percussion and other sounds, together with some ideas for using your musicians effectively.

Making a model is a good way to record facts learnt about the three families. It may involve some problem solving too. Making a 'prop' or something to wear helps to make a chosen role more real.

■ When you see the sign ![sign] turn to the pull-out pages for detailed suggestions to start you off on craft work. *These pull-out pages may be photocopied and enlarged.*

Clothing can help children feel more at home in a role. There is an illustrated clothing page for each family in the pull-put pages, with ideas for making clothes and accessories.

The cassette that goes with this book contains all the music played or sung, line by line, and then as an ensemble. Some of the music is played on instruments of the period and there are accompaniments which you may use as a backing track for your own singing or playing. For the **dances** there are voice-over instructions. The dances are fun to learn and provide a varied vocabulary of movement. Extended versions of the dance music on cassette may be used if live players are not available, or as incidental music for drama work.

Visual aids The shops at National Trust and English Heritage properties are excellent sources for picture postcards, slides, and posters. We also recommend the shops at the National Portrait Gallery and the Victoria and Albert Museum.

Parents

If you visit **historic properties** with your family, you will see at first hand different settings for family life in the past. The activities in this book can help to prolong the pleasure of your visit and to stimulate further interest in the way adults, children, and servants used to live. Have a good look at cooking equipment, for example, and at portraits on display. A list of properties to visit can be found on the inside back cover.

Then and now At first the three families may seem strange, remote from family life today, but after some discussion you may decide that, in essence, human nature has not changed very much. People no longer bow and curtsy, and boys and girls are more likely to share the same education, but there are still festivals and formal occasions, we still glamorize popular heroes like Dick Turpin, and enjoy a family outing to a street market or fairground.

History Skills

This cross-curricular approach to studying a period of history may seem complex, but in the process children acquire many useful skills, for example, the ability to consider cause and effect; to use contemporary texts, pictures, and music; and an awareness of social structure within a group of people. However you decide to **record** what you have learnt while working on these projects (visual displays, or perhaps as classroom drama), make a point of including music and dances because they express so vividly the spirit of their time.

Introducing
the Music

The music in this book is all **music for a purpose**: it can be played to create a mood, or to bring a personality to life. The Tudor *Pavane* expresses the dignified formality of the manor house when special guests arrive. *The Ratcatcher's Song* draws us into the robust company of the London street sellers. Each piece of music should have its own **distinctive character**, so the musicians are invited to make their own decisions about speed, style, and instrumentation. Make sure everyone understands the purpose of each piece before you start. The suggested instrumentation is just one possibility; try out ideas of your own, use your own resources.

Practical Tips

Experiment with beaters of different weights for percussion instruments. Try soft beaters and hard beaters. How many ways are there to play a tambourine? Perhaps a piece of scrap metal, or wood, or an empty tin will produce just the sound you want for the backing for a song. On the cassette, you will hear some home-made instruments of this kind, (street-scene sound picture).

Xylophone and guitar players–Mount written-out parts and see that they have a stand for their music placed where they can see it clearly. Use white wire library stands or home-made stands of stout card if music stands are in short supply.

Clarinets and trumpets–If you have players available, remember that they are transposing instruments. For them, and for violinists, it is best to consult the children's music teacher before writing out parts, to make sure the notes are ones they can find with confidence.

Recorders–Descant recorders and voices together make rather a harsh sound and singers may not be able to hear any mistakes in their intonation. Use a tenor recorder or xylophone if voices need support, unless you choose a shrill sound for a special effect.

Accompaniments–Before working out the accompaniment or backing for a tune, *everyone should be familiar with the melody*. This will help the backing players to keep in step with the tune by listening, rather than by counting inside their own heads regardless of anyone else.

Dance music–The steps dictate style and speed so everyone should learn them while the teacher plays the music, live or on cassette. Then, when their turn comes to play, the musicians will know how the music and dance steps fit together.

Sound pictures–Creating a sound picture is best done gradually, allowing time for discussion, and time to try out sounds; work on one 'section' of the picture at a time. Don't forget to devise a means of recording on paper, as you go along, what you have decided to do. Finally, you could perform your sound picture live in your drama, or it could be recorded on cassette.

1
A Tudor Family

*Here is a list of members of a Tudor family
and some of their servants:*

Sir Robert Bowman
father of the family and master of the household

Lady Bowman
mother and mistress of the household

The Bowman Children
Hal, Robin, Anne, Celia, and Eliza

William
their cousin

Master Hobson
steward of the household

Tutor to the children

Indoor Servants
Cooks, Maids of the Wardrobe, Yeomen of the Buttery,
Herbalists, Spitboys, Maids of the Pantry, Portrait Painters

Outdoor Servants
Falconers, Beekeepers, Farm-workers, Gardeners

If your drama work includes a visit from Queen Elizabeth I to
the manor house, someone will be needed to represent her, and
others to be her attendants.

Contents

A Tudor house with a knot-garden and members of the Bowman family. (*You may photocopy and enlarge this picture.*)

Sir Robert and Lady Bowman and their Steward

Sir Robert Bowman is an important man, Member of Parliament, and Lord Marshall for his county. At the time of the Armada he was responsible for seeing that his county's quota of men were ready with longbows and pikes to defend England if the Spanish army should land.

Lady Bowman runs the household. This is no easy task, as eight members of their family and twenty-five servants eat daily in the Hall and kitchen. All the food is produced by their own farm-workers and gardeners. Food has to be home-preserved against winter shortages; anything bought in the nearest town has to be fetched in wagons toiling along rough roads. The household is largely self-sufficient; they even have their own brewhouse and blacksmith's forge.

With the help of her maids, Lady Bowman tends a special garden of herbs to make pot-pourri and medicines, and to strew among the rushes on the floors.

Master Hobson is Sir Robert's cousin and Steward to the Household. He sees that the servants carry out the master's orders correctly.

The manor house is partly brick, partly timber-framed, built round an inner courtyard. Gardens and orchards surround the house, and nearby there are stables and farm buildings with thatched roofs.

An important Tudor gentleman like Sir Robert keeps among his servants his own band of musicians to play for various occasions: the arrival of honoured guests; dancing after a banquet; and for his family's pleasure at any time. They wear his livery and play stately music like the *Pavane* opposite in the Minstrels' Gallery above the Great Hall.

ACTIVITIES

Sir Robert and Lady Bowman
■ Make a table-top model of your house and gardens.
■ Paint a life-size portrait of yourself as a Tudor lady or gentleman.
■ Write some pages of your diary.

Steward
■ Make a medallion for your chain of office.
Make some Tudor money to reward good service, for example, some groats, nobles, and sovereigns.

Pavane *A grave and stately dance*

from Etienne du Tertre *Book 7, 1557*

Use a deep-toned drum to play this rhythm as a two-bar introduction, and then continue to play it softly and steadily throughout the dance.

Listen to the 'Pavane' played on instruments of the time, two treble viols and a bass viol. How does this version sound different?

Basic Tudor Dance Steps

Simple left = step sideways onto left foot and place right foot beside it (close).

Simple right = step sideways onto right foot and place left foot beside it (close).

Double left = take three steps: left, right, left, and close.

Double right = take three steps: right, left, right, and close.

Double forward = take three steps forward: left, right, left, and close.

Double backward = take three steps backward: right, left, right, and close.

Dance a Pavane

The Pavane may be danced in couples or threes. Play the music through once while gentlemen lead their ladies to their positions, well spaced out, with everyone facing the top of the Hall.

The dance begins and ends with a **Reverence**. This is a deep bow or curtsy to the master of the household, or whoever is the most important person present. The musicians must play a two-bar chord using the first note of each part for the Reverence. Dancers should move smoothly and hold their heads high; remember, fine clothes, starched ruffs, rich jewellery, and the importance of making a grand impression. The sequence is Reverence, drum introduction, dance, Reverence.

Make your Reverence, listen to the two-bar drum introduction, and begin:

Simple left, simple right, double forward (bars 1-4)
Simple right, simple left, double backward (bars 5-8)
(Remember, two steps per bar.)

The Bowman Children and their Tutor

There are five children in the family: Hal, Robin, Anne, Celia, and baby Eliza. William their cousin is being brought up with them, sharing their tutor and learning good manners. The girls share some lessons too, but also learn to sew, and to manage a household as their mother does, while the boys learn Latin, fencing, and falconry. All the children learn to ride well and exercise their horses in their father's park.

Sir Robert and Lady Bowman are fond of their children but very strict. Every morning the children must kneel to receive their parents' blessing, and girls as well as boys might be beaten for disobedience. When they are old enough to marry, the girls will be expected to accept their parents' choice of husband.

Everyone learns to dance and to sing; some can play the lute or viol, harpsichord or recorder. On rainy days they can dance and sing in the Long Gallery, or play indoor bowls or chess. On the following page is *The Horses' Dance* for the children to learn on a day when it is too wet to ride.

ACTIVITIES

Children
■ Invent a Tudor board game to play on wet days. It could be based on the Armada battles, or a game using dice, or perhaps a game like Snakes and Ladders.

Tutor
■ Make a Hornbook. If the Queen visits the manor, you will be asked to read an address of welcome. Useful phrases: 'Most gracious Majesty...', 'We, your loving subjects...', 'We have prepared for your delight...'. Finish with *Vivat Regina*! which means 'Long live the Queen!' in Latin.

The Horses' Dance

from Arbeau's Orchesographie, 1589

A light-hearted miming dance for the Bowman children

Use claves or a woodblock or coconut shells to accompany the recorders and make a sound like horses' hooves. Follow the rhythm marked with an 'x'. The dancers will want this music played briskly as they take two steps per bar. Remember to play a two-bar chord using the first notes of each part for a Reverence at the beginning and end of the dance.

Dance Steps

Form a circle, boys and girls alternately, and make your Reverence. Two bars on the claves will then set the speed before you begin (see page 10 for basic dance steps). Join hands and dance a double left (clockwise), then a double right (anti-clockwise), bars 1-4. Repeat this, bars 5-8.

Drop hands. Boys paw the ground twice with their left foot, like a horse, bar 9, then take a simple left, stamping their feet, bar 10.

Now, pretending to hold the reins of a restless horse, they turn round on the spot taking eight small steps, bars 11 and 12.

The girls now perform the same actions to bars 13-16. Repeat the dance and finish with a Reverence.

In contrast to the solemn *Pavane* this miming dance is cheerful and lively.

A Christmas Round

Traditional

Christ - mas is com - ing, the goose is get - ting fat; Please to put a pen - ny in the old man's hat!

This is a round for two, three or even four voices, if you can manage it. The voices enter at one-bar intervals.

When you have sung through four or five times, all the voices could join in this ending:

Please to put a pen - ny! Please to put a pen - ny! Please – a pen -ny!

Listen to the lute accompaniment. What other instrument does this remind you of?

Tudor Servants

Servants' Duties

Tudor servants were really skilled craftsmen and women, specializing, for example, in training falcons, cooking, bee-keeping, or work in the blacksmith's forge. In return for their skilful contribution to the household and farm, they were given a 'livery' or at least a family badge to wear, as well as board and lodging. Exceptional service was rewarded with a coin or two.

ACTIVITIES

Servants, Cooks, Falconers, Maids of the Pantry, Maids of the Wardrobe, Yeomen of the Buttery, Spitboys, Herbalists, and Miniature Portrait Painters.

Gardeners
■ Make a model knot-garden in a symmetrical design (see page 7), with flower-beds, a fountain, and clipped trees. Could you design a maze or a bowling alley?

Jack the Farm-worker's Song

from Deering's Country Cries, *c. 1600*

Father Jack **Father**

Jack, Jack, sleep'st or wak'st? Vast a - sleep, Fa - ther, Cham vast a - sleep, Fa - ther! O Jack, rise and

Jack

feed the cat - tle and the sheep! Nay, first chill ha' my break - fast, for all cham fast a - sleep!

Henwives (calling their chickens)

Tig, tig, tig, tig, tig, tig, tig, Coop, coop, coop, coop, coop, coop, coop, Bid - dy, bid - dy, bid - dy, bid - dy, bid - dy, bid - dy, bid!

This song is written in Elizabethan country dialect. *Cham*= I am, *chill*= I will, *vast*= fast. Make a strong contrast between Jack's voice, his father's voice, and the chorus of clucking henwives.

ACTIVITIES

Jack and his Father
■ Make a model cottage, timber-framed and with a thatched roof. Where will you place it in relation to the manor house on the table-top model?

14

A Beekeeper's Song

from Deering's Country Cries, *c.1600*

Voice 1

Ring out your ket-tle of pur-est met-al to set-tle, to set-tle the swarm of bees.

'Buzzers'

Voice 2

Buzz, buzz, buzz, buzz, etc.

Ring out your ket-tle of pur-est met-al to set-tle, to set-tle the swarm of

To keep you thriv-ing your bees must be hiv-ing, be hiv-ing, be hiv-ing, so no time lose to hive your bees.

bees. To keep you thriv-ing your bees must be hiv-ing, be hiv-ing, so no time lose to hive your bees.

The beekeeper and two or three assistants could invent an introduction for this song using their voices and various percussion instruments. First the bees come gradually out of their hive and make themselves into an angry swarm. Then the keepers make clattering noises (with kettles and pans) to scare them slightly, so that they will settle on a nearby branch and can be gently lifted into the clean hive that is all ready for them. Throughout the buzzing and clattering sounds, keep a rhythmical beat going on the note C, using a chime bar.

When the singers come in, this beat is taken up by the 'buzzers' who keep the buzz on middle C going throughout the song. It also provides the right starting note for voices 1 and 2.

Lady Bowman finds honey is a good sweetener for drinks and delicate puddings. She uses beeswax for her best candles and for polish. The family owns a number of hives, standing in the orchard, and employs a beekeeper to look after them.

A Tune for a Jester

from Mainerio Dances, *1578*

Someone in your Tudor household is sure to want to be a jester, so here is a tune for him or her. The musicians will enjoy making up an accompaniment using lively rhythms and lots of bells.

The staccato (dotted) notes provide a useful pattern to repeat, and the notes E and B will fit as a drone, played on a xylophone, chime bars or guitar (strummed E minor chord).

Elizabethan Poems and Texts

Sir Robert Sidney writes to a friend, describing the Queen's visit to his house in 1600 (this letter could inspire paintings by the children):

Her Highness hath done honour to my poor house by visiting me, and seems much pleased by what we did to please her. My son made a fair speech, to which she gave a most gracious reply...

The women did dance before her, while cornets did salute from the gallery. The Queen smiled at the ladies, who in their dances oft came up to the step on which the seat was fixed to make their Reverence...

She did eat two morsels of rich comfit cake, and drank a small cordial from a gold cup...

Two Ushers did walk before the Queen, and going upstairs she did call for a staff, and was much wearied by walking about the house, and said she wished to come another day.

Six drums and six trumpets waited in the court, and sounded at her approach and at her departure.

The French Ambassador, writing in his journal in 1597, describes Queen Elizabeth's accomplishments:

> *(The Queen) takes great pleasure in music and dancing ... in her youth she danced very well, and composed measures and music, and had played them herself and danced them. She takes such pleasure in it that when her Maids dance she follows the cadence with her head, hand and foot.*

A **measure** was a dance invented for a special occasion. Based on the simple and double steps, it included freer movement around the dancing space, couples meeting and crossing in symmetrical patterns, making their Reverences, all in the style of a *Pavane*. Could you, like the Queen, compose your own Measure?

A Nightwatchman's Song

Maids, to bed and cover coal,
    Let the mouse out of her hole.
Crickets, crickets in the chimney sing
    Whilst the little bell doth ring.

(The nightwatchman had a bell which he rang every hour on his rounds.)

2
A Stuart Family

Here is a list of members of a Stuart family, their household, and the people in the London streets nearby:

William Prosper
a London merchant

Alice Prosper
his wife

The Prosper Children
Nathan, Sophia, Joseph, and Lucy

Sue
a companion for Mistress Alice

Their **Three Maids**

Tom
a boy to run errands

Plague Doctors

and ten or more **Street Sellers**

If you decide to use the drama ideas you will also need street porters, a cutpurse, and some Press Gang men.

Contents

Pull-out pages contain ideas for Stuart craft, drama, and clothing

A Stuart town house (after the Great Fire of London) and members of the Prosper family. (*You may photocopy and enlarge this picture.*)

William and Alice Prosper and their Children

The head of our Stuart family is William Prosper. He started work as an apprentice and is now a rich merchant, trading in the rapidly growing city of London. England and Holland were at war in the seventeenth century and his ships ran the risk of being attacked and plundered. His seamen and workmen could be taken by force at any time by the Press gang to work in the King's navy.

Alice Prosper, William's wife, not only runs their household, but she knows enough about his business to take decisions when he is not there, and to advise him about what people will want to buy. She has four servants to supervise and at least ten people to cater for daily, and if anyone falls ill she nurses them. Alice is teaching these management skills to her daughters, Sophia and Lucy. The girls learn at home as they are not allowed to explore the busy streets alone like their brothers Nathan and Joseph. The boys walk daily to St Paul's School.

Tutors come to the house to teach the girls to read and write. The boys join them for lessons in music and dancing. Generally girls sing and play the harpsichord or spinet and boys play the recorder, flute, flageolet, or bass viol.

With easier access to shops and street markets there is no need for a Stuart household in London to be as self-sufficient as a Tudor household in the country.

Stuart Servants

The three maids would all do general household tasks (washing, cleaning, and cooking) rather than specializing, as in a Tudor household. Their days were spent sociably working together, and they would seize any chance to go shopping and so meet other folk in the streets.

ACTIVITIES

Prosper Family
- Make models of a merchant ship and the dockside
- Make a collection of different merchandise

Maids
- Bake some ginger biscuits

Nutmegs and Ginger

from an anonymous seventeenth-century consort piece

Buy my nut-megs and gin-ger!   Cin-na-mon, cin-na-mon and all-spice!

Cin-na-mon, cin-na-mon and cloves!   Fine to-bac-co, cof-fee and to-bac-co, Buy my nut-megs and gin-ger!

Try adding some light percussion to the chorus, 'Buy my nutmegs and ginger!' William Prosper trades in cane sugar and tobacco from the West Indies port of Bridgetown in Barbados. He sends ships to Portugal for wine, to North Africa for pepper and spices, and to Bombay for silks, calico, and indigo dye. He plans to buy coffee in bulk from Greece to supply the now fashionable coffee-houses.

A Pedlar's Song

from A Country Garland, 1687

I have the finest choice for you,
　　Both Ribbons, Gloves, and Laces,
With powder, paint, black patches too,
　　And masks to hide your faces.
A powder for your teeth I have,
　　My pretty maids now buy it,
The which will make you white and brave
　　If you will please to try it.

Song from a Play

Nose, nose, jolly red nose,
　　And who gave thee that jolly red nose?
Nutmeg and ginger, cinnamon and cloves,
　　They gave me this jolly red nose.

(These spices were mixed with hot ale to make a winter drink.)

ACTIVITIES

Cooks
■ The gingerbread tastes very good!

Gingerbread

Original recipe from *The Compleat Housewife* an early seventeenth-century cookery book.

Take a pound and a half of treacle, two eggs beaten, half a pound of brown sugar, one ounce of ginger beaten and sifted; of cloves, mace, and nutmegs all together half an ounce, beaten very fine, coriander seeds and caraway seeds, of each half an ounce, two pounds of butter melted; mix all these together, with as much flour as will knead it into a pretty stiff paste; then roll it out and cut it into what form you please; bake it in a quick oven on tin plates; a little time will bake it.

Look back to your collections of sugars and spices. Why are such large quantities used in this recipe? What type of heat was used for cooking and how was it regulated? Do you have to 'beat and sift' spices nowadays? For which important ingredient is no exact quantity given? Do you think this recipe is for a beginner or an experienced cook? Most seventeenth-century housewives made their own hand-written collection of recipes, though this printed book became popular.

Tudor Drama Ideas

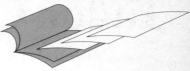

1. Queen Elizabeth I visits Bowman Manor

During the summer months, Queen Elizabeth I often travelled around her kingdom on a Royal Progress, visiting one large house after another. Sir Robert Bowman would receive news of her impending visit by letter, a rather startling letter to read out to his wife. What preparations will be necessary? How will he entertain this formidable monarch and her many attendants?

Having decided together what to prepare, Sir Robert, Lady Bowman, and Master Hobson might share out the task of visiting the outdoor and indoor servants at work, and making sure everything is being done well.

As the servants set about their tasks they can sing *Jack the Farm-worker's Song* and *A Beekeeper's Song*.

The Queen is at the gates! She must be greeted with solemn music, and seated on a splendid chair. The Tutor reads his address of welcome (see page 11). Yeomen of the Buttery bring refreshment. Maids of the Pantry bring her favourite sweetmeats on special roundels. She enjoys dancing, music, and receiving gifts, e.g. a flattering portrait, a trained falcon.

A ragged figure creeps dangerously near the Queen's jewel box, placed by the royal chair. Catch him! Catch him! What shall be done to such a villain: the stocks, an even sterner sentence, or a merciful pardon?

To smooth over such an unfortunate happening the Steward, almost at his wits' end, remembers the Jester. So the entertainment ends happily, and the Queen retires to music.

2. A Tudor Christmas

Traditionally, the Great Hall would be decorated with holly, ivy, and evergreens for the twelve days of Christmas. The woodmen dragged in a huge yulelog and poor people of the parish expected alms (*A Christmas Round*). Some might be old seamen who had sailed with Sir Francis Drake or fought in the Armada battles, with tales of adventure to tell. Games like 'Blindman's Buff' were popular, and there was a strange topsy-turvy custom: two servants, chosen to be the Lord of Misrule and his Lady, sat in the place of honour, and were waited on by the Master and Mistress and their family. The children might entertain the company with *The Horses' Dance*. When the feast is over someone could recite the poem 'Maids, to bed...' (see page 17).

Tudor Craft

Sir Richard Bowman's Diary

Write a diary of a journey to London. Mention the condition of the roads. Did he ride through forests, cross rivers by bridge or ford, change horses, and stay overnight at an inn, meet beggars or robbers, stop to visit a fair? Were there any other adventures? Could you make him a route map?

Lady Bowman's Diary

These are examples of events you could record: a fire in the kitchen, a visit from a pedlar, a child falls ill, finishing some embroidery, making six jars of apricot preserve.

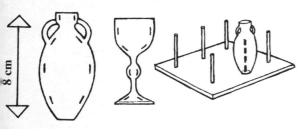

Yeomen of the Buttery (Butlers)

Here are some patterns for jars and goblets. Cut out two of each shape in light card. Staple them together. Use a wooden tray covered in silver foil. Make holes in the tray and fix dowels or sticks so that the wine jars stand up.

Tudor drinks include sac, ale, fruit cordial, mead, and Rhenish wine. Find out how the drinks were made; which were home-made, and which were imported.

Spit Boys and Kitchen-maids

You will need a pole to represent a spit, about 120 cm long. Cut out two of each of these shapes, and staple them together so that they can be threaded on the pole. Colour them with wax crayons to give a nice roasted appearance.

Arrange a support for each end of the spit, and make a crêpe paper fire beneath it.

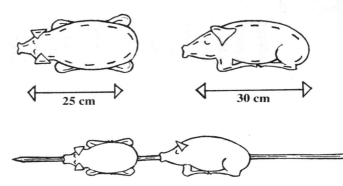

25 cm 30 cm

A Miniature Portrait

Draw a 5 cm circle on white paper. Using fine felt pens, draw a brightly coloured portrait of the Queen inside it. For the mount, cut a 10 cm circle of card. Decorate round the edge with macaroni, etc. stuck on and sprayed with gold, and with sequins. Paste the portrait in the centre of the mount and attach a ribbon to hang it round your neck.

My first is in . . .

A Roundel

Maids-of-honour Cakes

You will need:
1 large packet of puff pastry
125g of castor sugar
100g of curd cheese
125g of butter or margarine
40g (about) dry breadcrumbs
2 egg yolks, 1 lemon, 1 pinch of nutmeg
25g of ground almonds, or semolina with two drops of almond essence

What to do:
1. Roll out pastry thinly and line about 24 bun tins with it.
2. Cream butter and sugar together.
3. Add all other ingredients, with juice and grated rind of the lemon.
4. Place one teaspoonful of the mixture in each pastry case.
Bake at 350° F (180° C) or Gas Mark 4 for about 15 minutes.

Stuart Drama Ideas

1. Will the Press Gang catch you?

William Prosper and his head clerk stand at one side of your work area. At the opposite side, a huge cart of merchandise newly unloaded from one of the Prosper ships has just arrived. As the clerk reads out from his list 'Five barrels of wine from Portugal!' or 'A crate of Barbados sugar!', the porters carry, or trundle, or heave the heavy goods across the street and into the warehouse. Make sure the bystanders realize how hard it is for them. Some singers could cheer the work on with *Nutmegs and Ginger*.

Tom has been down at the docks on an errand. He hears people whispering 'The Press Gang are coming!', and he knows the porters are all out in the street. What must he do? And quickly!

2. Shopping in a London Street

Against the background of your sound picture of London streets and the Street Cries, Mistress Alice and her daughters go shopping, with Sue in attendance. They are fussy customers, but the shopkeepers and street sellers are eager to sell. Along come Nathan and Joseph, dawdling on their way to school. Quick! A cutpurse has stolen Mistress Alice's money! 'Stop thief! Stop thief!'

3. The Story of the Great Fire

Nathan and Joseph have found a Sun Insurance fire-sign in the street. They show it to their father, who explains what it is. They are both too young to remember the Great Fire, so he and Alice tell the children what happened, and how they felt when they learned that their own house was to be blown up to make a fire-break. They explain that the house was rebuilt in brick. Sophia asks her mother what she saved from the house and why. Her father tells Lucy what he ran back to rescue. Use the song and sound picture of the Great Fire to accompany the story.

4. Remembering the Plague

Mistress Alice describes the danger from the Plague the year before the fire and shows the children one of the herbal bags she made to ward off infection. She describes how finally she took the children to the countryside and left William on his own. What might Sue have to say about how her family fared in a poorer, overcrowded part of London? Do the Prosper children wish they had been older then? (This situation lends itself to flashback treatment).

Stuart Craft

Prosper's Merchant Ship

Make a cut-away picture of a merchant ship, showing the holds where sacks and barrels of merchandise can be stored. Don't forget the ship's galley, the captain's cabin, some guns and a sailor or two.

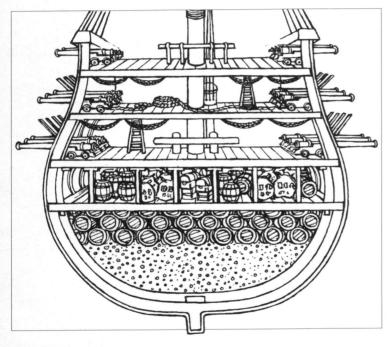

London docks

Make a model of the dockside showing sacks of spices, barrels of sugar, chests of tea, chocolate and coffee, bales of cotton, coiled ropes, all to scale, and add any other dockside objects you can think of.

Plague Doctors

1. Fill some small muslin bags with strongly-smelling herbs and spices to keep away infection, especially the plague.

Pound the herbs and spices first, using a pestle and mortar. Hang your herb bag round your neck on a loop of wool.

2. Make a large poster to put up all over London warning against the plague, e.g. all cats and dogs must be killed (but dogs killed rats, so was this sensible?); all plague victims must have a red cross on their doors; no victim was to come out of their house; and everyone must chew tobacco!

3. Some doctors were cheats or 'quacks'. Make some 'pretend' plague cures with fancy names like 'Dragon Water' or 'Venice Treacle'.

Street Sellers

Make trays to display your cowcumbers, vegetables, hot spiced gingerbread, oranges (rare and expensive), and anything else you can think of.

Collections of Merchandise

Collect different kinds of merchandise.

1. Sugars: barbados, demerara, granulated (modern beet sugar), etc.
2. Drinks: some were introduced in Stuart times, i.e. tea, coffee, chocolate.
3. Materials: silks, velvet, brocade, cottons, linen, flannel.
4. Spices: cloves, peppers, cinnamon, ginger, nutmeg, mustard.

Make a clearly labelled display of each collection.

Georgian Drama Ideas

You could display your large painting of the Fairfield house and park as a background for your drama.

1. A Masked Ball

Two pieces of music will be useful here. Play the *Grand Minuet* as guests arrive and greet one another with well-polished bows and curtsies. The masks should cause amazement and surprise, fans can be flourished. When the second piece, *Music for a Masked Ball,* is played, you could make up a formal dance of your own, with partners and symmetrical patterns. How will you finish this scene; with a country dance or refreshments?

2. Stand and Deliver!

Sir Frederick Fairfield's coach is stopped by highwaymen. How will Lady Georgina react? What will the two footmen who ride behind the coach do? The coachman has a blunderbuss under his seat. The highwaymen carry pistols and are very cocky so they do not bother to watch what the coachman is up to. Sir Frederick is just about to hand over his gold watch and his Lady's jewellery when...!

You could start with the coach arriving at a toll-gate and Sir Frederick giving the coachman the correct money for the toll collector. The Highwayman's Song would make a good ending. You could make a blunderbuss, pistol, and gold fob watch.

3. Harvest Home

Every year when the harvest is safely gathered in, Sir Frederick provides a feast for his tenants and farm-workers. Anyone who has a song to sing (*The Shepherd's Song, The Fox Song*) can entertain their friends, a tenant farmer recites the 'Farmer's Poem', everyone joins in the country dancing (*A-Hunting We Will Go*).

4. Christmas time in a Georgian Household

The Fairfield children would be expected to entertain their parents and their friends with music (*A Duet for Two Treble Recorders*) and poetry (the poem about the dormouse).

They may show their embroidery, or painted fans, or their new watches and brooches to the company. Carol singers from the village are announced, and after performing *A Christmas Song*, are led down to the kitchens for refreshments by the governess.

Georgian Craft

A Fan for a Georgian Lady

Cut in half lengthways a piece of sugar paper (60 cm x 42 cm). This will make two fans. For each fan paint a bold design, with birds, flowers, or fish perhaps. Keep your design to the top 15 cm of the paper. Fold each paper in concertina fashion, each fold about 2 cm deep. Press the folds together so that for each fan you can make a handle by stapling the bottom folds and binding with sellotape. Now open out your elegant fans!

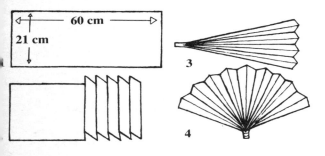

Farmer's Poem

Let the wealthy and great
   rule in splendour and state
I envy them not, I declare it.
I eat my own lamb, my own chickens and ham,
I shear my own fleece and I wear it.
I have lawns, I have bowers,
   I have fruit, I have flowers,
The lark is my morning alarmer;
So jolly boys now, here's God speed the plough,
Long life and success to the farmer!

Governess

Make a set of skittles. Collect nine plastic squash bottles and fill them equally with enough sand to make them stand upright but still be fairly easy to knock over with a ball. Rules for the game might include a fixed line to throw behind.

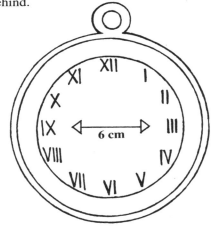

A Watch for a Georgian Gentleman

Cut a disc of cardboard 6 cm in diameter, with a knob at the top. Cover with gold paper or spray paint. Draw a watch-face on a smaller circle of white paper using Roman numerals and glue it into position. Crochet a watch-chain from string and spray it gold. Drill a hole in the knob and attach the watch-chain. A fob watch fit for Sir Frederick Fairfield!

Poem. Written by a little girl on the death of her pet.

In paper case, hard by this place,
   Dead a poor Dormouse lies;
And soon or late, summoned by fate,
   Each Prince, each Monarch dies.
Ye sons of verse, while we rehearse,
   Attend instructive rhyme;
No sins had Dor to answer for;
   Repent of yours in time.

Sewing Maids

A sampler gave girls practice in embroidering letters and numbers so that they could name and date their linen. They added designs for trees, birds, flowers, etc. Use bright wools, a tapestry needle, and broad-weave canvas, if you are a beginner.

Highwaymen

Make a highwayman's mask. Cut out the mask shape in black card. Reinforce the holes and attach round, black elastic.

For a Masked Ball

Cut out your mask in coloured card and decorate in spectacular fashion with feathers, sequins, beads, etc.

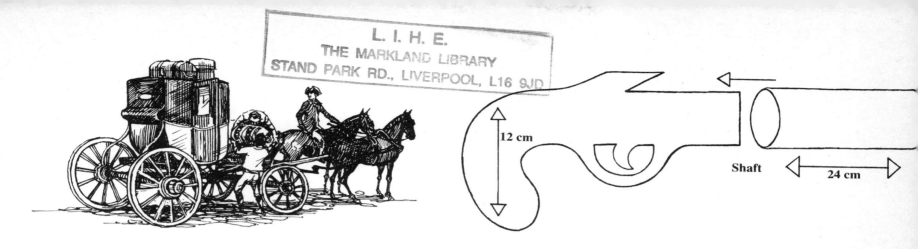

12 cm

Shaft

24 cm

A Toll Notice

FOR EVERY HORSE, MULE, OR ASS, LADEN OR UNLADEN, AND
NOT DRAWING A CART, THE SUM OF..........................1d

FOR EVERY HORSE, MULE, OR OTHER BEAST DRAWING ANY
WAGON, CART, OR CARRIAGE, THE SUM OF..................4d

FOR EVERY DROVE OF CALVES, SHEEP, LAMBS OR PIGS, PER
SCORE, THE SUM OF...5d

Draw up your own toll notice.

'A score' was twenty. What did '1d' mean? Can you work out a toll
for this carriage? Vehicles with narrow wheels paid higher tolls as
they damaged the road surface.

Lemon Syllabubs

Take a small carton of cream, or small tin of evaporated milk. Whip
it until it is thick, stir in 75g of fine sugar, and the rind and juice of a
lemon. Then pour into individual glasses and let them stand 5 or 6
hours, or you may prefer to leave them overnight before serving.

These pages may be photocopied by the purchaser only.

Pistol and Blunderbuss

To make the pistol, find a cardboard tube about 24 cm long. Measure its
inside diameter exactly. Draw and cut out the handle and trigger shape in
stout card, with the shaft exactly as wide as the tube's diameter. Ease the
shaft into the tube or barrel of your pistol. Paint it. For a blunderbuss use a
longer tube.

Georgian Clothing

Georgian gentlemen wore white shirts with a white cravat. Tuck trousers into white socks to make britches, and disguise modern shoes with buckles made from foil and cardboard. Waistcoats were important: make a false front for a man's waistcoat using furnishing brocade or braid decorations, and sew on bright buttons. Disguise a modern coat by giving it deep turnback cuffs, and add braid and very large buttons down the whole length of the front. Hold the coat open with a half-belt at the back to display the waistcoat.
Sir Frederick might wear a modern wig, tied at the back with a black bow, and a felt hat with the brim turned back. **Boys** wore similar clothes to their fathers after the age of ten. Before that they wore long coloured trousers with a white shirt, ruffled at the neck, and their hair short and uncovered.

Working men wore a natural or self-coloured shirt, a white or coloured neckerchief, a plain waistcoat, britches, grey socks and plain shoebuckles. **Farmworkers** wore smocks: try a man's shirt worn over trousers, with 'smocking' drawn on the chest with a felt pen, and a red hanky knotted underneath the collar. Add boots and a very battered, old felt hat, well pulled down. Keeping face and hands clean would not be easy.

Ladies' dresses of the late Georgian period are easier to contrive than the earlier, wide-panniered designs. Favourite colours were white or pale pastels, so an adult nightdress worn over a full petticoat, and pulled in to a high waist with a sash, should produce the right silhouette. Add a white kerchief or ruffled collar, and more ruffles at the wrists. Long hair can be piled up and decorated with a flat white cap with ribbons or a straw hat with a generous bow. A black ribbon round the throat looks elegant. **Girls** wore the same style of dress but with short sleeves so again a nightdress is useful, with a very wide, pale pink or blue sash.

Women servants wore a self-coloured blouse and long skirt, white cuffs turned back, a plain white neckerchief, and a long white apron. Add a white mob cap, discreetly ribboned.

Special touches: highwaymen wore a black handkerchief tied round the lower half of their faces; ladies of fashion wore one or two black beauty patches on their faces; Sir Frederick would wear his watch in his waistcoat pocket, the chain draped across his front.

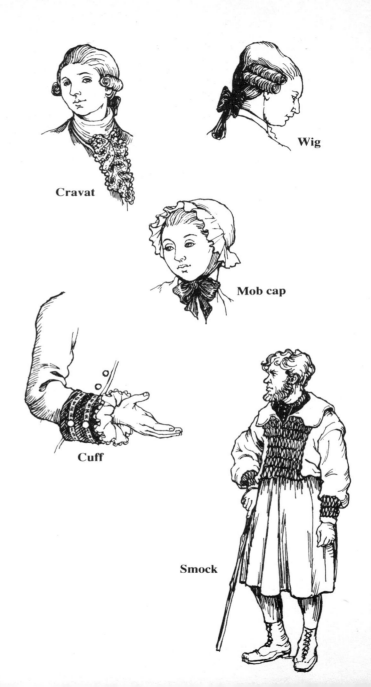

Cravat

Wig

Mob cap

Cuff

Smock

The Great Fire

Make a table-top model showing the Great Fire. In the foreground make a model of the River Thames, with boats, London Bridge, and houses on it. As a background, make card silhouettes of the houses, warehouses, old Saint Paul's, etc. Use torches or wired (battery) circuits for red flames. How could you show houses blown up for fire-breaks? There could be some on your bridge.

A Frost Fair

Make a picture or collage, including skating figures, an ox roasting, sledges, dancing bears, carts, and booths. See page 29 for an extract about a frost fair from John Evelyn's diary.

Ginger Biscuits

A seventeenth-century recipe, adapted for today.

You will need:
2 full tablespoons black treacle
1 full tablespoon golden syrup
120g moist brown sugar
1 beaten egg
355g plain flour
1 teaspoon each of powdered ginger and cinnamon
½ teaspoon each of powdered cloves, nutmeg, coriander, and caraway seeds
225g melted butter
Currants or walnut pieces for decoration

Mix all these ingredients together in a bowl with a wooden spoon. Gradually add the flour to make a soft dough. You will need extra flour to sprinkle as you cut the dough into biscuit shapes or gingerbread men. Decorate with currants or walnut pieces. Bake on a floured tin for about 15 minutes at Gas Mark 6 or 400° F (200° C). Cool on a wire tray.

Sun Insurance Fire-sign

Copy this sign; you could draw and paint it, or make a poly-block print. Use it as a prop for Stuart Drama ideas, no. 3. If you bought a fire-sign like this one from an insurance company, they would send their firemen to your aid if your house was on fire.

These pages may be photocopied by the purchaser only

Stuart Clothing

Although members of the King's court and the nobility wore very elaborate clothes towards the end of the seventeenth century, **William Prosper's** clothing would be plain in colour and design, but of good cloth. Find him a long coat and cover the buttons with silver foil. Turn modern trousers into britches by tucking them into long white socks. Add a white shirt, a waistcoat, and a broad-brimmed felt hat. **Working men** wore britches too, tucked into long grey socks, with shirts, waistcoats, and a black or coloured kerchief knotted under the chin. Make your own kerchief by tie-dying an old piece of sheeting about 40 cm square. William Prosper's necktie would be a strip of fine white material tied in a single knot. The **Prosper boys**, like Tudor boys, would wear simpler versions of their father's clothes.

Alice Prosper's gown would be long and of rich material, perhaps silk brocade woven by the French craftsmen in Spitalfields. Ladies' sleeves were elbow-length with white cuffs, and a white scarf or strip of lace called a 'whisk' was worn round the shoulders. Pearl necklaces and earrings were fashionable. Out of doors, Alice would wear a black hood or scarf loosely covering her head. Her **daughters** would have similar dresses, although protected by a short apron, and would not be allowed jewellery.

Maidservants would wear long aprons over dresses of plain material and a white cap, but a spirited girl could add a piece of lace or ribbon to make herself more stylish. Maids had white hoods to wear outside.

Collect ribbons for William Prosper to wear as garters with full bows on the outside of the leg, or as shoe decorations. Alice and her daughters would wear ribbons round their sleeves.

London was always short of water and people who worked in the streets could not easily keep clean. Make the **street sellers'** faces and hands dirty, and give them battered old hats to keep off the weather.

Necktie

Black hood

White cap

Ribboned sleeve

Gown

Maids of the Wardrobe

Cut out this shape in light card to make a bowl for pot-pourri to perfume the Queen's bedroom. Decorate with flower patterns, and make a portrait of the Queen in the centre with felt pens. Fold up each of the four sides and staple together to make a bowl.

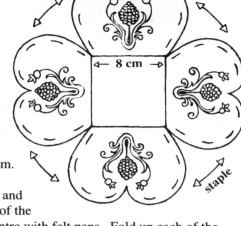

Maids of the Pantry

Make a roundel or sweetmeat plate. Cut out a circle of thick card about 18 cm in diameter. Decorate it with coloured flowers, birds, and fruit. In the centre write a riddle. On the back of the roundel write the answer.

Herbalists

1. Collect a few small jars to hold a salve for chapped hands; mix a few drops of rosemary or almond oil into some plain handcream. Turn the salve into a chest rub to ease a cough by adding drops of eucalyptus oil.

2. Collect fresh herbs in season. Which are used for cooking, and which are valued for their aroma? Label them, and write decorated labels for your salves too.

Falconers

1. Cut out each of these four shapes twice, using thin card.
2. Staple a wing to each body.
3. Staple the two body pieces together, leaving a gap for stuffing with tissue paper. Staple handle pieces together, tuck into body, and staple in position.
4. Staple sides of the hood together. Add a crêpe paper tassle and bright decorations.
5. Paint your falcon; a bird book will show you the colouring of different species.

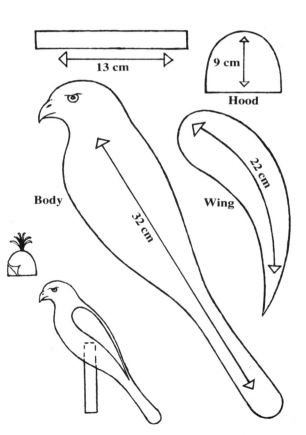

Tutor

Make a hornbook to teach the Bowman children their alphabet and the Lord's Prayer. The writing was protected from the children's grubby fingers by a thin sheet of horn; use a piece of clear plastic. The frame and handle were made of wood; but you could use painted card.

These pages may be photocopied by the purchaser only.

Tudor Clothing

Trousers tucked into coloured socks make good britches for **gentlemen**, with a ribbon garter tied below the knee. Modern shoes may be disguised with a lace or plain, black ribbon shoe-rosette. A short cloak helps a gentleman like Sir Robert Bowman to swagger a bit, as befits his station. Gentlemen also wore ruffs and caps. A jumble sale beret or velvet toque, with a brooch added to one side, would do well.

Servants wear their trousers tucked into grey or white socks, and smart white collars. An outdoor servant needs an old felt hat, brim turned down. Some servants need aprons, not too clean, where dirty hands have been wiped on them. Falconers need a gauntlet each to protect their hands and spit boys need a sweat-rag around the neck.

Ladies like Lady Bowman move with dignity in long skirts. A bum-roll, worn beneath the skirt, pads it out like a farthingale, and low necklines were fashionable with a ruff to show off a pretty neck. Long hair can be pinned up and a lace mat, held in place with grips, makes a neat cap. Crescent-shaped shoulder pads were worn by both men and women; make them in material to match the jacket or bodice, and decorate with gold or silver braid, and beads.

Servant girls dressed like their mistresses or as close as they dared, but in plain colours. They wore white coifs on their heads and long white aprons.

Tudor portraits show children wearing smaller versions of their parents' clothes. Do you think they were ever allowed to take off the more cumbersome garments when playing? Girls wore their hair loose or with a lace-trimmed coif, boys had a flat cap with a feather. Borrow a black academic gown for the tutor and find him a flat black cap.

Bum-roll

Ruff

Coif

Shoulder pad

A Sound Picture of London Streets
in the Seventeenth Century

Street Cries

OLD RAGS! OLD RAGS!
BUY MY COWCUMBERS, READY TO PICKLE!
HOT SPICED GINGERBREAD!
FINE YOUNG RABBITS!
HAVE YOU ANY WORK FOR KIND-HEART THE TOOTH-DRAWER?
HERE'S A FINE NEW BALLAD!
FRESH SPRING WATER!
WHO'LL BUY MY APPLES, WHO'LL BUY MY PEARS?
ROW YOU OVER THE RIVER, SIR OR MADAM!
CURES FOR ALL YOUR ACHES AND PAINS!

1. Choose two or three favourites from the street cries and make up a snatch of tune for each one (using three notes at the most). Vary the rhythms to fit with the words. It's best to keep to one key. If the key is G, for example, you can use the notes G, B, and D. Keep the cries in tune by strumming a G on a guitar or chime bar.

2. Now make up a backing of street sounds for your cries, e.g. hurrying feet, heavy horses, nimble ponies, squeaking rattling carts, chattering voices, etc.

How noisy the streets of London must have been! If you had to shout out all day, 'Who'll buy my apples, who'll buy my pears', you would find it helped to 'chant' the words, perhaps like this:

3. Join the backing and street cries together to make a sound picture. Be careful to vary the street sounds and keep to just one or two cries at a time, or you will end up with a jumble of sounds.

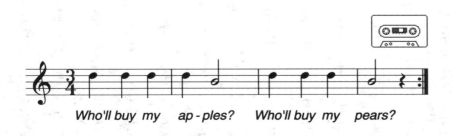

Who'll buy my ap-ples? Who'll buy my pears?

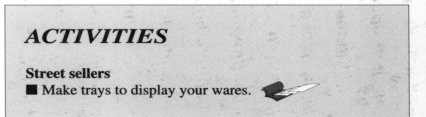

ACTIVITIES

Street sellers
■ Make trays to display your wares.

The Plague in London, 1665

Samuel Pepys was famous during his lifetime because he helped to build up King Charles II's navy. He is still famous today because he kept a diary. He recorded both day-to-day happenings in his household and dramatic national events, such as the Great Plague of 1665. Here is an extract from his diary:

July 20th 1665

Walked to Redriffe, where I hear the sickness is... there is 1,089 died of the plague this week. My lady Carteret did this day give me a bottle of plague-water to take home with me... grass grows all up and down Whitehall Court and nobody but poor wretches in the streets.

Doctors could find no medicine to cure the Plague. The ratcatcher was more effective than the doctors because the fleas which spread the sickness lived in the fur of black rats. The more he killed the less the plague spread.

A Sound Picture of the Great Fire, 1666

Here is part of a poem about the fire which Pepys bought from a ballad seller in the street. It mentions the blowing up of houses to make a fire-break.

The second of September, in the middle time of night,
In Pudding Lane the fire began to burn and blaze outright.
With hands and feet, in every street men pack up goods and fly,
Pitch, tar, and oil increase the spoil, old Fish Street 'gins to fry.

From Sunday morn 'til Thursday night it roared about the town,
There was no way to quell its might but to pull houses down;
And so they did, as they were bid by Charles his great command;
The Duke of York, some say, did work with a bucket in his hand.

1. Read these verses aloud together until every word is understood and audible.

2. Now compose a backing to accompany the ballad. List the sights and sounds to be included: the wind that spread the flames, the thick smoke, the crackling timber... What about explosions, nearby or far off?

3. Choose instruments or sound effects for each item on your list.

4. Give your sound picture a shape or form. Remember it started in a small baker's shop. Let it rage between the verses, but the words themselves must still be audible. The strongly marked rhythm of the verses might give you a basic pattern to work on. Which of you will speak the words?

How will you finish? With houses being blown up, or with the flames dying away to silence?

The Ratcatcher's Song

from Deering's Country Cries, c.1600

Rats or mice, rats or mice, rats or mice? Have you an-y rats, mice, pole-cats or weas-els, Or

have ye an-y old sows sick of the meas-les? I can kill them, and I can kill

moles, And I can kill the ver-min that creep-eth up and creep-eth down and peep-eth in-to holes.

Guitar chords are provided above the melody. You could also add a xylophone part using these notes.

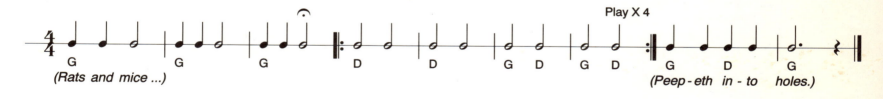

(Rats and mice ...)

Play X 4

(Peep-eth in-to holes.)

ACTIVITIES

Plague Doctors
- Make a herb bag to ward off the plague

Great Fire
- Make a model of the Great Fire
- Make a Sun Insurance fire-sign

A New Year Carol

from New Christmas Carols (*Oxford Book of Carols), 1642*

The old year now a - way is fled, The new year it is en - ter - ed, Then let us now our

sins down - tread, And joy - ful - ly all ap - pear. Let's mer - ry be this day, And

let us now both sport and play. Hang grief, cast care a - way, God send us a hap - py new year!

2. Come maid and man, come Tom and Sue,
   Come drink to your Master and Mistress too,
   Our feast is spread, our grace is said,
   So joyfully all appear.

   Chorus: *Let's merry be* etc.

Notice the use of the bass viol for accompaniment.

New Year's Day was more of a feast day in the seventeenth century than it is now; a day for the master of the household to provide a special dinner for his servants, and for everyone to settle their debts and make good resolutions for the coming year.

We have written the second verse especially for the Prosper family. Could you make up a third verse?

Fear No Danger *A trio for three recorders*

from Purcell's opera Dido and Aeneas

The Prosper children could play this trio to entertain their parents' guests. Instrumental music was usually performed in a private, home setting, but in London the very first public concerts were being held at this time.

Play the first eight bars of the descant 1 part as an introduction. Then play through the whole piece: A, B, A, C, and A once more.

Goddesses *A country dance*

from Playford's The English Dancing Master, *1651*

Listen to the different versions of this on the cassette. Which instruments can you hear?

King Charles liked to dance these 'country dances of Old England' at court, so the Prosper family would probably dance this in quite an elegant though lively fashion.

Dance Steps

Form two lines, four boys on one side, four girls on the other. Keep to just eight dancers, otherwise there will be a scramble to fit the steps to the music. Of course, more than one set of eight can dance at the same time. Look back to page 10 to remind you of the steps (Simples and Doubles).

Figure 1: All face spectators and dance a double forward, and a double backward. This takes the first four bars of the music, two steps to a bar. Repeat for bars 5-8.

Chorus: Both lines cast off, dance down the set, meet at the bottom, and the first couple lead their lines up to the top again (bars 9-16).

Figure 2: First man leads his line round the women's line and back to their places. Chorus as above.

Figure 3: First woman leads her line round the men's line and back to their places. Chorus as above.

Figure 4: Men join hands in a ring and dance round, returning to their places by bar 8. Chorus as above.

Figure 5: Women join hands in a ring and dance round, returning to their places by bar 8.

Repeat Figure 1, and Chorus to finish. Remember to bow and curtsy to your partners at the beginning and the end of the dance, to a two-bar A minor chord.

ACTIVITIES

■ Make a picture or collage of a frost fair

A Frost Fair, 1684

Here is an eyewitness account by the diarist, John Evelyn:

...The frost continuing, more and more severe, the Thames, before London, was still planted with booths in formal streets, all sorts of trades and shops, furnished and full of commodities even to a printing press, where the people and ladies took a fancy to have their names printed, and the day and year set down when produced on the Thames...at sixpence a name. Coaches plied from Westminster to the Temple and from other stairs, to and fro, as in the streets; sleds, sliding with skates, or bull-baiting, horse and coach races, puppet shows and interludes, cooks, tippling and other lewd places; so that it seemed to be a carnival on the water.

3
A Georgian Family

Here is a list of members of a Georgian family and some of their servants

Sir Frederick Fairfield
a country landowner

Lady Georgina Fairfield
his wife

The Fairfield Children
Richard, Henry, Caroline, and Mary

The Tutor

The Governess

Sewing Maids

Cooks

If you decide to use the drama ideas, you will also need farmers, guests at a Ball, highwaymen, etc.

Contents

Pull-out pages contain ideas for Georgian craft, drama, and clothing.

A Georgian house and grounds, and members of the Fairfield family. (*You may photocopy and enlarge this picture.*)

Sir Frederick and Lady Fairfield
are wealthy landowners

Their country house stands in a spacious park, and beyond that there are farms let to tenants. Although their house is large (twenty-five rooms for the family and a separate wing for the servants) they are following the fashion and building on improvements: a grander front entrance, a new coach house, and stables. The park is being landscaped to extend the view from the house. The rooms within contain fine furniture, books, pictures, and statues in Classical style.

Polite Manners

In wealthy Georgian society, manners are very dignified. Lady Georgina teaches her daughters, Caroline and Mary, to make deep, elegant curtsies. Her sons, Richard and Henry, learn from their Tutor to bow gracefully, removing their hats and holding them against their chests. They also learn to stand when a lady enters the room, and to step aside with a bow to allow her to pass through a door first.

ACTIVITIES

Children
■ Practice your polite manners while the *Grand Minuet* is played. Music helps to set the tone and keep your movements unhurried. Here are some useful phrases to practise, 'Your servant, madam/sir', 'I thank you, sir/madam', 'I wish you good day, sir/madam'.

■ Paint a large picture of the Fairfield house and park. Include some builders, gardeners, and Sir Frederick and Lady Georgina admiring their improvements. The picture could be used in your drama work.

Grand Minuet

from a minuet by Grano, 1731

Drum rhythm: (for *Minuet* only) Use this pattern as an introduction and throughout the *Minuet*. In the *Turkish Trio* use lots of jangling sounds, e.g. tambourines and bells.

A 'musette' was a little set of bagpipes. That is why the *Musette* has a drone accompaniment; play it on chime bars, or violins using open G and D strings played together. For contrast, a smaller group of recorders could play the *Musette* melody. Play the *Minuet*, the *Musette*, the *Minuet*, the *Turkish Trio*, and finally the *Minuet* again.

The Fairfield Children and some Servants

Richard Fairfield, the eldest son, will inherit his father's house and lands. Henry may become a clergyman, or an officer in the army or navy. Aged ten and twelve, they now have a tutor in charge of their general education, including Latin and music.

Caroline and Mary are cared for by a governess, who teaches them to read and write, to sing and to play the harp or harpsichord. She supervises their play and takes them down to the kitchens to learn some delicate cookery or up to the attic sewing room. Lady Georgina plans to find them husbands from families similar to their own. She is teaching them how to run a large household and how to entertain guests with polite conversation and elegant meals.

All four children learn to ride, and enjoy some freedom out of doors. Perhaps the stable-boys taught them to sing *The Fox Song*?

Georgian Servants

A large number of servants were necessary for the Fairfield household, as in a Tudor manor. They were specialists, covering a wide variety of skills. Butler and Housekeeper top the list in importance, with Cook and Head Coachman next, and so in strict order down to the Kitchen Maid and Stable Boys. However, the servants' wing could be a sociable and lively community. Although this house, like the Tudor manor, stands in the depths of the country, improved roads mean that goods can be bought in the nearest town and transported more easily. The household need not therefore be so self-sufficient.

ACTIVITIES

Children
■ Learn to bowl a hoop outside and to race with it.
■ Make a fob watch, a brooch, or a fan.

Tutor
■ Find out about Dr Edward Jenner from an encyclopaedia so that you can teach your pupils about vaccination against smallpox. Do you think Lady Georgina would allow her children to be inoculated?

Governess
■ Make your own set of skittles.

Cooks
■ Make lemon syllabubs.

Sewing Maids
■ Embroider samplers, with the Fairfield daughters.

The Fox Song

Traditional

2. He came at last to a farmer's yard,
   Where the ducks and geese declared it hard
   That their sleep should be broken and their rest be marred
   By a visit from Mr Fox-o!

3. He took the grey goose by the sleeve,
   Said he 'Madam Goose, now by your leave,
   I'll take you away without reprieve,
   And carry you off to my den-o!'

4. Old Mother Slipper-Sloppers jumped out of bed
   And out of the window popped her head,
   'Run, John, run, the grey goose has gone
   And the fox is off to his den-o!'

5. John ran up to the top of the hill,
   And blew a blast both loud and shrill;
   Says the fox 'That's very pretty music, still
   I'd rather be home in by den-o!'

6. The fox sat down with his hungry wife;
   They did very well without fork or knife;
   They ne'er ate a better goose in all their life,
   And the little ones picked the bones-o!

Guitar chords are provided above the melody. Recorders: the last four bars can be played as an introduction to each verse, then join in the singing. A touch of crisp rhythmic percussion here and there will keep the song lively.

Fox-hunting was a favourite sport for the gentry, but this song describes how the fox himself went hunting; a good story to mime.

Music for a Masked Ball

from a Gavotte by Handel

Descant

Treble

Tenor

Sir Frederick Fairfield and his family go to a Masked Ball in a nearby town. They travel in his carriage, using the newly-surfaced turnpike-road. Travellers had to pay for the use of such roads; the money or toll was collected at a toll-gate. At the ball there will be formal dances such as Minuets and Gavottes, followed by more rumbustious country dances to round off the evening.

The musicians for the ball would most likely be self-employed professionals. Although some families made their own music at home, public concerts were quite frequent. Musicians could now find employment in the theatres, opera-houses, and assembly rooms, as well as private households.

The Highwayman's Song

Traditional

Guitar chords are provided above the melody. Coconut shells make a good sound for horses' hooves. Recorders: play this introduction before each verse, then join the singing.

1. As I was rid-ing o-ver the moor I saw a law-yer just be-fore, I rode up to him and this I did say 'Have you seen Dick Tur-pin ride this way?' With my her - o, Tur-pin her - o, O he is the val - i - ant Tur-pin— o!

Rich men's coaches ran the risk of being stopped on a lonely stretch of road by highwaymen on horseback. Brandishing pistols, they would demand money, gold watches and jewels. If caught, the highwaymen were sentenced to hang. Jack Ketch (verse 5) was a famous hangman. The song tells the story from Dick Turpin's point of view, who was thought to be quite a glamorous hero as well as a thief! His mare Black Bess became a national heroine for so bravely trying to save her master from being caught by leaping a toll-gate bar.

ACTIVITIES

Fairfield Family
■ Decorate a mask for the ball or make a fan
■ Draw up your own toll notice for the turnpike-road
Highwaymen
■ Make a highwayman's mask and a pistol

2. No, I've not seen Turpin for many a long day
Nor do I wish to see him ride this way,
For if I do I have no doubt
He'd turn my pockets inside out,
    With my hero etc.

3. They rode till they came to a powder mill
Where he told the lawyer to stand still,
Saying 'The tails of your coat they must now come off
For my mare she's in need of a new saddle cloth',
    With my hero etc.

4. Now I've robbed you of all your store
You can go and whistle for more,
The very next town that you ride in
Tell them you've been robbed by Dick Turpin,
    With my hero etc.

5. Dick Turpin was caught and his trial was passed
And for a game cock he was caught at last,
Five hundred pounds he gave so free
All to Jack Ketch as a small legacy,
    With my hero etc.

The Shepherd's Song

Traditional

How de-light-ful to see, in those ev'-nings of spring, When the sheep are all go-ing to fold, The shep-herd sings as he goes on his way, And the dog goes be-fore them when told, And the dog goes be-fore them when told.

Xylophone

Introduction (v. 1. only)

A G F A C' B♭ A G F C F

Verse

F F A A F

C' G C' B♭ C' C F A C' A G F A C' B♭ A G F C F

2. *Now as for those sheep, they're delightful to see,*
They're a blessing to a man on his farm.
It's the best of all food, for their flesh it is good,
And the wool it will clothe us up warm. (twice)

3. *Now the sheep are all shorn and the wool carried home,*
Here's a health to our master and flock,
And if we should stay till we all goes away,
I'm afraid t'will be past twelve o'clock. (twice)

A-Hunting We Will Go *A country dance*

Traditional

This tune is easy to play on either descant recorders or violins. Add some percussion to the long notes in bars 2, 4, and 8. The traditional words to this song are 'A-hunting we will go, a-hunting we will go, we'll catch a fox and put him in a box, A-hunting we will go!' Listen to the difference between the violin and dulcimer accompaniments.

Elementary violins play:

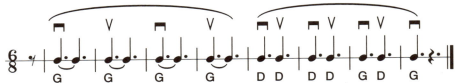

Dance Steps

Form a longways set: two lines, boys one side, girls the other, facing partners.
1. Top couple join hands, slip down to the bottom of the set and back up again.
2. Top couple cast off both lines and dance to the bottom, then make an arch with their arms. The other couples follow them down, pass under the arch and dance up to the top again.
3. First couple remain at the bottom of the set. The second couple now become the new top couple and the dance begins again.
Arrange the dancers in sets of no more than six couples; longer sets will leave the recorder players breathless!
SIR ROGER de COVERLY, a more elaborate country dance, can be performed to this same tune, and is described on the cassette that goes with this book.

Georgian Farming

Georgian landowners took a lively interest in farming: cattle and pigs were bred for size, and sheep to yield either more mutton or thicker fleeces. Turnips and other winter feed were cultivated. Sir Frederick has a home farm and several tenant farmers on his land. He is proud of his prize animals, his good crops, and especially of his shepherd and his flock. His farm labourers reckon the beasts are better fed and housed than they are. They used to be able to graze a cow or keep pigs on the village common land. Now Sir Frederick has enclosed most of the common to improve his farm. How do you think the labourers feel about this?

A Christmas Song

Traditional

Sir Frederick Fairfield's farm-hands and their families call at the big house hoping for something warm to eat and a drink by the blazing open fire in the kitchen. This is a song for them to perform for the master and mistress.

Guitar chords are provided above the melody. They could also be used as a xylophone part, if you prefer.

Notice the use of dulcimer for accompaniment on the recorded version.

2. Master and mistress, a-sitting by the fire,
   Pray think upon poor travellers a-travelling in the mire,
   For 'tis your wassail, etc.

3. Master and mistress, are you so well a-pleased
   To set upon your table a white loaf and a cheese?
   For 'tis your wassail, etc.

4. Master and mistress, without any fear,
   ♫
   I wish you a Merry Christmas and a Happy New Year,
   For 'tis your wassail, etc.

A Duet for Two Treble Recorders

from a Minuet by Lully

Richard and Henry Fairfield could play this duet. Notice that the breathing marks help you to phrase two bars at a time. Listen to this duet played on the harpsichord. What modern instrument does this sound similar to? How does it sound different?

Topics to Expand and Discuss

Tudor Family

Portraits–Look at a variety of Elizabethan portraits, including some of Queen Elizabeth herself. Why is it so difficult to find portraits of ordinary working folk? How did the artists convey grandeur and wealth in a picture?

Childhood–Do you think boys were valued more than girls? And if so, why? Was family discipline too strict?

The Queen on Progress–During hot summers she visited large country houses to avoid plague-ridden London. Compare with the present-day appearances of our royal family.

Cottages–Do some research into natural materials and methods of construction. Do any such buildings survive in your area? If not, why not?

Hunting and Falconry–Make a list of animal foods found in a Tudor forest, e.g. deer, wild duck. Why did people hunt, especially in winter? What was the falcon trained to do? Was there ever a forest in your area?

Stuart Family

Ships–Do some research into ship-building: types of vessel, navigation, trade, and discovery. Why was the Press Gang necessary?

Town Planning–After the Great Fire, buildings were made in brick, streets were built to a plan. Find out about Sir Christopher Wren.

Materials–Compare the difference in feel between real silk and modern rayon; cotton and nylon; wool and man-made fibres. How were materials made, washed, and cared for?

Imports–Use an atlas to find the source of coffee, real silk, port wine, cotton, dark-brown sugar.

City Streets–Find out about rubbish disposal, buildings overhanging the streets, open shop fronts, horse-drawn traffic, and nightwatchmen. Imagine the sounds of a busy street.

Communications–How would Sir William Prosper send a message to one of his managers south of the river? Discuss the importance of Tom as a messenger on foot because there was no telephone, and only a limited postal service. The River Thames was used for transporting goods and people.

Health and Hygiene–Find out about the supply of drinking water in those days, beginnings of scientific research, the Royal Society, and Sir William Harvey. It's now known that the plague bacillus was carried by rat fleas. How would this knowledge have improved health conditions?

Fire-Fighting–Why was it difficult to put out the Great Fire with seventeenth-century equipment? Discuss the dangers of wooden buildings, open coal and wood fires, hay, pitch, tar, and oil stored in the streets.

Georgian Family

Road System–Find out about the construction of roads, tolls, stage-coaches, the improvement of carriages, and easier communications.

Farming–Look into the changes made in farming, e.g. winter feed and who gained and who lost by the enclosure of commons and open fields. Look for pictures of improved animals bred for size.

Fox-Hunting–Why did the gentry go fox-hunting so enthusiastically? They employed special hunt servants: grooms, huntsmen, and gamekeepers. Compare Georgian fox-hunting with Tudor deer-hunting, and falconry.

Manners–Discuss the value, or otherwise, of formal manners. Compare Georgian formality with manners today, for example, how do motorists, customers and shopkeepers, and children behave? How could clothes indicate social position? Does this still happen today?

Music and Family Life and the National Curriculum

This book provides ample opportunity for National Curriculum implementation. Listed in the charts below are the relevant Attainment Targets for six of the National Curriculum subjects, for each section of the book. The photocopiable 'pull-out pages' also contain further possibilities for drama and craft activities.

■ TUDORS	MUSIC	HISTORY	ENGLISH	P.E./DANCE	TECHNOLOGY	ART
Sir Robert and Lady Bowman and their Steward		1, 2	1, 2, 3, 4, 5		2, 3	1
Pavane and *The Horses' Dance*	1, 2			✓		
The Bowman Children and their Tutor		1	1, 2, 3		2, 3	1
Jack the Farm-worker's Song	1, 2	1	2		2, 3	
Tudor Servants and *A Beekeeper's Song*	1, 2	1	1, 2		2, 3	
A Christmas Round and *A Tune for a Jester*	1, 2					
Elizabethan Poems and Texts	1	1, 3	2	✓		
■ STUARTS						
The Stuart Town House, the Prosper Family, and Servants		1, 3	1, 2		2, 3	1
Nutmegs and Ginger	1, 2	1, 3				
London Docks and people in the streets		3			2, 3	1
Seventeenth Century London Streets and Street Cries	1, 2		1		1, 2, 3	
The Plague in London, 1665, and *The Ratcatcher's Song*	1, 2	1, 2, 3	1, 2		1, 2, 3	1
The Great Fire, 1666	1, 2	2, 3	1, 2		2, 3	1
A New Year Carol	1, 2	2, 3	2, 3, 4			
Fear No Danger and *Goddesses*	1, 2	1, 3	2	✓		
Stuart Poems and Texts	1, 2	1, 2, 3	2		1, 2, 3	1
■ GEORGIANS						
The Georgian House, the Fairfield Family, and Polite Manners		1, 3	2	✓		1
Grand Minuet	1, 2					
The Fairfield Children and Servants		1, 3	2		2, 3	1
The Fox Song	1, 2	3				
Music for a Masked Ball	1, 2	1, 3	2		2, 3	1
The Highwayman's Song	1, 2	1, 2, 3	2		2, 3	1
The Shepherd's Song	1, 2	1, 2, 3	2			
A-Hunting We Will Go	1, 2	3		✓		
A Christmas Song and Georgian Servants	1, 2	1, 3				
A Duet for Two Treble Recorders	1, 2	1				